Alistair Bryce-Clegg

FROM VACANT
TO ENGAGED

Putting child-led learning at the heart of your planning

Published 2012 by Featherstone Education
Bloomsbury Publishing plc
50 Bedford Square, London,
www.bloomsbury.com

ISBN 978-1-4081-6398-6

Printed in Great Britain by Latimer Trend & Company Ltd
10 9 8 7 6 5 4 3 2

This book is produced using paper that is made from wood grown in
managed, sustainable forests. It is natural, renewable and recyclable.
The logging and manufacturing processes conform to the environmental
regulations of the country of origin.

To see our full range of titles visit **www.bloomsbury.com**

Acknowledgements

We would like to thank the following staff and children for their time and patience
in helping put this book together, including the use of a number of photographs:

Acorn Childcare Ltd

St Thomas Moores Primary School

The Friars Primary School

Marlborough Road Primary Schools

The Arches Primary School

J.H Godwin Primary School

Blackpool LA

Saint Andrews Primary School

Middlefield Primary School

Noah's Ark Pre School

Crofton Hammond Infant School

Hampshire LA and their Leading
Foundation Stage Practitioners

Contents

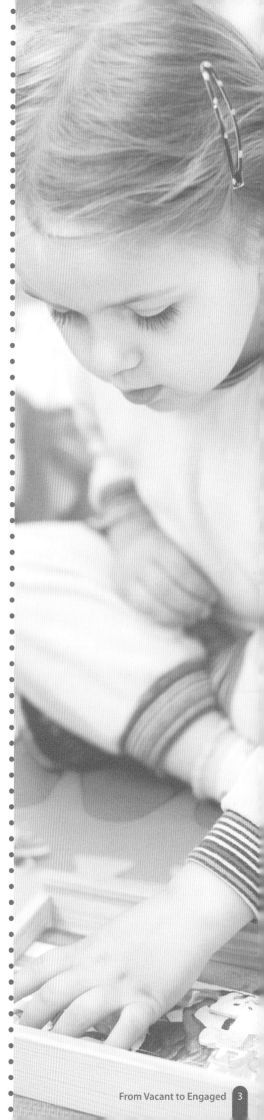

Introduction 4

Chapter 1: Creating an engaging environment 6

Where do I start?
Keeping the space alive
Skills development
Stages in mark making development
An environment plan

Chapter 2: Display 10

Where to start
Where should I display?
Speech bubbles and captions
Learning stories
A scrap book display – The Gruffalo

Chapter 3: Continuous provision 24

Mark making
Assesment information
'Dressing' your provision
Challenge tubes
Process NOT end result

Chapter 4: Role-play 32

Deconstructed role-play
The role of the adult
Small world play

Chapter 5: Planning for engagement 36

Step 1: Assessment
Step 2: PLODS
Step 3: Responding to children's interests

Chapter 6: Engagement through creativity
Case studies 40

Case study 1: Project CSI
Case study 2: Project Fairy folk
Case study 3: Project Outdoor space
Case study 4: Project Bones
Case study 5: Project Deconstructed role-play
Case study 6: Project Den making

An environment plan 62

Introduction

I was lecturing to some student teachers and at the end of the session one of them asked me if I could produce a list of the things that I thought made a 'good' teacher. Initially I started my response by saying that there was not just one thing that made a good teacher but that good teaching came from a collection of attributes most of which took a lot of time and effort to acquire.

First of all I think it is essential that **you like children**. You may think this would be a foregone conclusion but my years of experience as a pupil and then working with teachers tells me otherwise!

Then there is **subject knowledge**. The more you know then the more you are able to put in place to help children to learn.

Not forgetting **experience and all of the knowledge** and 'tricks of the trade' that a few years in teaching could bring. I say 'could' because we are all familiar with the teacher who has been teaching for 20 years but has taught the same group 20 times, rather than learning from 20 different ones.

You need to have some **passion** for the job because it's hard work and the demands of children can be very draining on top of all of the other 'stuff' that is required of teachers these days.

It then struck me, that although all of these things were very valuable attributes when working with children, none of them on their own would make you a 'good' teacher. I have worked with people who had outstanding subject knowledge but were not great teachers, people who had taught for donkey's years but still weren't great and I know teachers who are extremely passionate about what they do but that passion doesn't transfer into their teaching.

The one thing that is missing from my list is the most important. Unlike the others it is the one that you cannot acquire, you have either got it or you haven't. The best practitioners, whatever their qualifications, are the ones that have got it in spade loads. Without it you'll find yourself fighting a losing battle a lot of the time.

What is it? Engagement. If you can engage children in their learning then most of the hard work is done. Then, following on from this, the more you know and the more experience you have will help you to have even more of an impact on children's learning and attainment.

Rather than just being the *receivers*, children should be the *discoverers* of their learning. We, as practitioners, have the very difficult and clever job of teaching children things that they don't know (and that they probably don't want to know, given a choice) and convince them it was their idea in the first place! Easy.

Alistair Bryce-Clegg (ABC)

Creating an engaging environment

Whatever the size and shape of your space, your environment has the potential to have a significant impact on children's levels of engagement. The key is to make sure that children feel ownership of the space and that how you have arranged the resources and the content of your display are for the children and not you.

When thinking about planning for your environment, it's important to remember that it encompasses both indoors and out. Outdoor provision is such a crucial part of the EYFS curriculum that it should receive equal weighting in terms of planning and resourcing as indoors. Unfortunately, it is often the poor relation and the lack of provision results in a huge number of missed opportunities, especially for those children who it can be harder to engage (did somebody mention the boys?)!

A good early years environment will always have a healthy amount of child-generated mess on any given day. The odd handprint on the wall, splash of paint on the lino and unidentifiable brown stain on the carpet! Notice that I said 'child-generated' mess. There is a significant difference between the mess that children make when they are engaged in a learning process and the sort of mess that adults leave lying around. We are creating and maintaining a learning environment for children. Any adult 'stuff' should be filed or piled in a cupboard or drawer and not left on display for all to see.

Where do I start?

So where do we start with creating an engaging environment? First you need a blank space and I mean blank! When the previous children have left you and moved on you need to strip everything back. My general rule of thumb is that nothing should go on the wall that hasn't been made by an adult or a child in the setting at the time. If you want maximum engagement with your environment, then you need the children to create it from scratch so that they can feel ownership and involvement. So, everything comes down: number lines, alphabets, colour recognition charts, even the birthday balloons (radical, I know!). Then in the first few weeks when the children are getting used to you and you are assessing what they can do, that is when you will create all of your everyday display – with them, for them. More information about this later!

Once you have stripped your space back to basics, you need to think about how you will put it back together again. The main tool to use for this exercise is any assessment or observation information that you have gathered about the children who are about to arrive. If you haven't got any, then use your knowledge of general point of entry attainment of previous cohorts and child development expectations in the key areas of learning. If I had no information about the children at the time of set up I would create a very 'loose' structure and be aware that I would be doing some shifting around once the assessments started to come in.

Assuming that you have got some assessment and observation details, then you need to use that information to base the structure of your environment on. As no two cohorts of children are exactly the same, then no two environments are going to look exactly the same even with the same resources in the same space. Your space should respond to the needs identified by your assessments.

Look at the assessment information you have and identify what, for this cohort, is the main inhibitor to learning. This is where you are going to place your main focus both in terms of space and resources. Children's ability to take on information and learn is directly in proportion to their feeling of well-being. If they are unhappy and unsettled then they are not in a learning frame of mind. To this end, consider how your space is helping to ease the transition. Have they got a space that is theirs? Are routines simple and well practised? Are there familiar objects/ photographs that are a link to familiar people and places that might help to reassure them?

If your data indicates that 'talk and language development' is an area of weakness, then you need to shape your environment to reflect that. First, work with your team to identify which areas of your space and which resources have an obvious impact on talk like role-play and small world play and then think about how you can encourage the development of dialogue in the way you structure and place your resources.

If 'talk' is your main inhibitor to learning then you might well create a specific designated 'talk area' where you can work on children's specific issues and gather resources for significant impact.

I will often ask a setting if they can show me their most recent summative data and then walk me around their environment pointing out how it has been structured and enhanced to meet the need identified by the assessment.

Top Tip from ABC

In one setting I worked with, we gave all the children four clear wallets that hold visitors badges (just don't tell the office manager!) and asked families to provide photographs of people that were significant to the child. We put the photos in the wallets and then joined them all together on the end of a plastic belt clip. This meant that each child could keep close a collection of familiar faces to look at if they were feeling a little anxious. Some of the team were concerned that the sight of a loved one, even a photo, might make the children more upset. But, I have to say that the opposite was the case and the children absolutely loved looking at their own and each other's photographs.

Keeping the space alive

Of course, this need will change as the children's skills develop. Your learning space should not look the same in September, as it will in July the following year. At the beginning of the year, you would expect to see large areas and resources given over to the development of emerging skills. As these skills become more and more refined, then more space and resourcing would be given to consolidating these skills and so on.

I am a firm believer that a good EYFS environment should be fluid. By that I mean that children should be able to take resources between areas and not be restricted to 'between these two sets of shelves is our mark making area'. Or that adult voice that bellows across the setting; 'Stop! Freeze! What is that in your hand young lady? I thought so…play dough! Get it back to the dough table. You almost went on the carpet… and you know what happens when we get dough on the carpet…' Unfortunately, I have never heard the end of that phrase so I am not quite sure what the answer is!

If I have a lump of dough and I want to take it to the workshop and stick some fandango feathers in it and then take it into the role-play as my pet – then I should be able to do that. We are supposed to be creating environments that allow children to learn through play-based discovery and well planned activities. You can't learn much if everything has to stay within a metre square area. Also young children will be displaying perfectly normal developmental behaviours like transporting objects – that is the nature of children's development and they should be allowed to do it!

Skills development

I think that it is often a very good idea to consider the skills that you want to develop with the children and then roughly zone areas that have key impact on those skills. Say we were thinking about mark making. Often, the mark making area will consist of a set of shelves with some nice resources on it and a table to write on. But the development of the ability to mark make and then write is far more complex.

If you consider what skills a child needs to be able to begin mark making, the list ends up being quite a long one. Most children start with a mark making implement gripped in their hand and they use their chest and shoulder to power their (often straight) arm. If we are helping and encouraging children to develop this early emergent skill then we need to think about what we've got in our setting that would help chest and upper body development alongside coordination. This is one of the few things that practitioners find it easier to plan for outside because there are usually lots of things for children to climb on, pick up or roll. Inside, it can feel a bit trickier but the principal is the same. Look for activities indoors that really work that upper body. One of the best things is working large lumps of dough for gross motor and smaller lumps of dough for fine motor – so is your dough area near your mark making table?

Stages in mark making development

- When children are gripping their mark making implement and using their shoulder to power their arm, then the marks they make will probably be big ones as they are not bending their elbow or wrist to make a smaller pivot. Have you got large spaces for children to do that large scale mark making inside and out? Is there an opportunity to do it near to your dough area?

- When they get a more well developed upper arm then they will begin to pivot at the elbow and the wrist making their marks smaller and more accurate. Is there a table top space or floor space to support this development?

- As they advance even further, children will begin to move their mark making implement out from their fist and towards the end of their fingers where they will be perfectly placed to begin to triangulate their grip. Have you got resources on your shelving that support this stage of development?

- In terms of skill development that will help with mark making, they could probably do with some practice in developing hand/eye coordination, low load control (shoulder's ability to support the arm during mark making) and some work on proprioception (how the body functions within the available space).

Painting/mark making on a vertical surface is very good for developing these skills. So are blackboards and easels near to the mark making space as well as in other parts of your setting? Does your space tell a story of skill development as well as creating opportunities for exploration and a good dollop of awe and wonder? Is your main role-play near to your small world, construction and talk area? All of these 'basics' can have a very positive impact on talk.

An environment plan (see pages 62-64)

Ideally you want children to feel free to move resources around the setting so they are not stuck in one place, but also you should be creating little pockets of experiences everywhere to enhance any 'moments' that arise. You need to provide opportunities to mark make and problem solve and offer little baskets of books linked to an area of interest or play that will encourage the children to use books in a real situation. Practice should be multi-layered and skill development opportunities should appear in as many different guises as possible to give a higher chance of engagement.

At the beginning of the year you can use your assessment to identify your key gaps. Once you have those as a priority list, then you can arrange your setting (indoors and out) to reflect a heavier weighting in space and resourcing for your key areas of development. Now within all areas you look at the skills that you need to develop and make sure that there is enough appropriate resourcing to support that development. The environment plan is a way of recording all of this information. It should be done in bullet points and kept really simple.

Top Tip from ABC

I encourage all of the settings that I work with to complete an **environment plan** (see pages 62-64) every year. It's a very simple document to put together but it's useful in clarifying with the team why their setting looks the way it does. It provides a clear link between assessment and the environment and it clearly shows how you have changed the environment in response to children's needs.

Display

As a newly qualified Reception teacher (or 'probationer' as we were then referred to as!) I used to spend hours and hours dressing my classroom for 'impact' – or so I thought! Every board was backed in a different colour with a contrasting border. I backed my room within an inch of its life and I backed in every material imaginable; tin foil, wrapping paper… the list goes on. I always thought, the bigger, the brighter, the better. I thought that that was what young children needed to see – lots of lovely bright colours to get their interest. Looking back now, I think that it was probably more about what I thought my classroom said about me and how good a teacher I was rather than how it was impacting on children's well being and learning.

Lots of settings I visit suffer from this 'chocolate box' syndrome where the walls are pretty and bright but they have very little impact on learning. One thing that is very different in today's classroom, that wasn't around when I first started teaching, is access to computer-generated, ready made, universal, downloadable display (or CRUD for short!). Now, don't get me wrong, I think the sites that produce this sort of thing do have some invaluable resources that no matter how creative you are or how much time you have, you couldn't make yourself. Some of these resources can make superb additions to your every day planning and provision. Where I despair is when settings have literally plastered their walls in sheets and sheets of laminated CRUD. Often in the same font with the same style of illustration and the same coloured background, making discrimination between them virtually impossible!

There seems to be a downloadable label for everything from drawer labels to role-play characters. I even saw one for the 'spare pants' box, which was kept in the storeroom! Because there is a label for everything, seemingly some people feel obliged to label every space so rooms become festooned. Any time a space becomes available we feel obliged to download a sheet, laminate it and stick it up quickly before someone notices! How many hours of their lives have poor TA's lost to being locked in a stock cupboard with a laminator and mountain of pouches being instructed in a 'Rumpelstiltskinesque' way to turn them into a display by dawn!

When I finally get to meet the children I just ask them about what is on the walls. What is it? Who did it? Do they use it? Often (not always) the answers to those questions are: don't know, don't know and no!

Alongside resources, good display is a key to maximising engagement. It should be made by children for children and should feature all of the things that they need to know most. This doesn't always look as pretty to some adults!

Top Tip from ABC

When I'm in a setting and I'm considering the impact of their display, I have a couple of general rules of thumb. Without looking at any planning, talking to any staff or children, just by looking at the walls can I get a real sense of the children who inhabit this space? Can I see the diversity of their curriculum, their interests? Is there clear evidence that the children's voices are being recorded and that they are shaping the content of the curriculum? Is there space around the display that really highlights the key features and is it personalised for THIS cohort of children?

Where to start

First step for me in preparing a display is a neutral background. Something that is a million miles away from what I would have done all those years ago! You want the children's work to really stand out from the wall that it is mounted on, not compete with it. A good test is to stand back from a display board and scrunch up your eyes. If all you see is the colour of the backing paper shining out then you have got the balance wrong.

As time has gone on, my preference for backing colour has gradually faded into magnolia (or maybe a light beige). White is too stark but cream for me is just about right. I want the board to disappear into the wall (I have often been known to paint them cream as well)! But, a word of warning, if you mount light coloured work onto a light coloured wall what you get is something that no-one looks at because it disappears. This is where your artistic flare can come in i.e. how you present that work, how you back it and how you place it. More on that later.

I've already said that what we are aiming for is that the space becomes personal to this specific cohort and does not contain lots of meaningless leftovers from last year and a few number posters from 1994 – so at the end of the year everything comes down and I mean *everything*.

No alphabet lines, no number lines, no key word displays, no instructional display – nothing! Just clean, bare, well-backed walls. I was once working on this idea with a setting and went in during the summer holidays to help them. The idea of completely stripping everything was met with absolute horror. One Reception teacher just kept repeating the word 'everything?' in disbelief. When she eventually managed to say 'what, even my birthday balloons?' and my response was 'yes, even your birthday balloons...'. She had to take herself off to the toilet for a 'moment'! The birthday balloons were clearly just one step too far for her at that moment, but I am pleased to report that (eventually) it all worked out well!

The other reaction I often get to this suggestion is 'what about the poor children?'. Well, what about them? And why have they all suddenly become poor because there is no alphabet line on the wall? I have even been told that it is 'cruel' not to have a 'lovely, bright environment' for them to walk into.

So, can I just clarify… no one said that it could not be lovely or bright. You are going to have exciting activities on your shelves: play dough that smells of strawberries and glitters, exciting small world sets, a choice of paints, a workshop area that is like a visit to Willy Wonka's chocolate factory, huge squashy cushions, a gazillion story books, felt tips, crayons, pencils and pens… The list goes on! It's just that your walls are going to be neutral – a blank canvas waiting to be filled. And when that first piece of work goes up, there it will shine out like a beacon and all who look upon it should get very excited and want their work to be up there too!

The day a child walks into a setting I'm working with and pronounces that they cannot work in it because it is too dull and demands the phone number of Lawrence Llewellyn-Bowen then I might rethink this approach!

Next step is to ask yourself what are young children motivated by more than anything else? More than Ben 10? More than sweets? Themselves! They are ego mad. They love nothing better than to see themselves in a video or in a photo. So if we are trying to create a display that will really motivate and engage them in their learning – a display that they want to interact with and return to, what should we use in that display? You got it – them!

There are all sorts of ways that you can use children's images in display and bearing in mind that you have just stripped all of your walls, we had better get started at exploring some possibilities.

Ben

What should I display?

I see lots of children's creations stuck up on walls. Once the child has completed their work of art, some adult has gone through the routine of 'Oooh, that really is fantastic! Now then, do you want to take that home (where it will probably be stuck a) in a pile, b) on the fridge or c) in the bin? OR, do you want me to put it on our amazing 'wall of pride' where everyone in the whole world will be able to see how spectacular you are? The 'wall of pride'? Are you sure? I wouldn't want to be seen to be influencing your decision…yes? Brilliant!'. So up it goes, with the child's name duly printed, laminated and stuck next to it which is great – apart from the fact that if I am 4 years old I might well be able to recognise my name, but I can't read so I don't know anyone else's and they don't know mine. However, if you stick *my photograph* up alongside my name then everyone knows it's me and I also get the self-esteem of seeing my face up on the wall.

One setting I worked with had the photographs stuck onto pegs with the child's name underneath. This made their storage and access easy. When the child's work went up the peg was just clipped on to it wherever there was a suitable gap. It worked really well.

Top Tip from ABC ✓

What I usually try to do is have about half a dozen laminated photographs of each child's face and when they have done something that you or they want to put up on the wall (or wherever) I dispatch them off to get one of their photos which goes up first before their name.

Another photographic initiative that I have worked on with great success is the personalised alphabet and number line. What self respecting EYFS setting doesn't have a number line and alphabet frieze? It is part of the essential kit! The question really is, how many of the key children who you need to target ever independently look at said alphabet frieze or number line?

As adults, we are like children in a sweet shop when it comes to these classroom essentials. There are so many to choose from. When I began my career you could only buy them from the Early Learning Centre and everyone had the same. Now, with the advent of the computer download there are literally hundreds of options.

How many four-year old August born children are really interested in and motivated by 'an apple'? Ah, but never fear because close on the heels of that stimulating fruit there is 'a ball' and then, like a gift from heaven… 'a cat'! Could there be anything less inspiring or motivational?!

Personalised alphabets and number lines

Sometimes, I see alphabet lines that are themed around characters that remind practitioners of their past. I saw one the other day with a very famous bear on it. The whole thing was in beautiful pastel shades of yellow. Now you would think that me being a self-confessed beige lover would be right into that. Well I'm not! The problem is, that apart from the lack of engagement for your key audience – it all looks the same. Now to our sophisticated eye, that isn't a problem but, if you are in the early stages of letter discrimination and everything is in the same font with the same background and the same style of illustrations then it makes your job of discriminating between q, o, p, a, d, b, c, and e even harder. After all, they are all just a combination of a bit of a circle that sometimes has a bit of a stick that sometimes goes up, sometimes down, sometimes left and sometimes right. It is little wonder our children get so confused.

The answer? Personalise them with children's photos. More importantly personalise key teaching displays to the children you are targeting with that knowledge – *not* the ones who already know it.

Top Tip from ABC

The key is to remember who we are buying them for, and the answer is, not you! They are going to be a key component that you will use everyday in your work to teach children the basic skills of Literacy and Mathematics. There will be some children who pick up these skills relatively quickly and easily, with or without the use of the alphabet frieze and number line, but there will be others who struggle, who have a little longer to travel down their path of development. So, when it comes to considering who we are targeting with this sort of classroom display, the answer is - the 'hard to reach' brigade.

My name is Alistair and if you were in my early years class, you would know that because the teacher was always shouting it out! If my teacher wanted to create a personalised alphabet, then where better to start than with me? I am going to love it and my classmates are going to be far more interested because it's not some animated apple, it's me! (Preferably sticking my tongue out for the photo as this will make the children laugh and raise the level of engagement even further!)

Make the photos nice and big. If you get to a letter of the alphabet and there is no one in your class or group who's name starts with that sound then ask the children what they would like to put in the picture? Remember if it's an alphabet line that you are using to teach initial sounds then you can't have 'Charlotte' for 'C' or 'George' for 'G'. It has to be the sound not the name. They will come in handy later on when you start doing blends.

With your number line, use assessment to identify who knows what in terms of number recognition. Then create your line by targeting the children who don't know to be in the photos. Make your most difficult to engage number 1! Trust me, it works wonders.

Child height display

I know that it can sometimes be difficult due to white boards, sinks and plugs but you should always aim to get your key displays at child's eye line height – not two metres up the wall near the ceiling! Young children don't usually look up unless they are prompted to do so by an instruction or a sound. They tend to look straight ahead and down at their feet. It helps them to keep their balance. If you want this display to have an impact on attainment then make it from a subject that they will be interested in and put it where they can see it.

I often find myself musing over the value of a laminated colour splat and what one of those ever taught anyone! When you create your colour recognition display, make it personal and make it interesting. There is nothing more boring than seeing a load of 'red' objects that you are not allowed to touch being pulled out of a feely bag by an adult and placed on the 'red' table, especially if I know all of my colours and I have to sit and listen to the adult witter on!

Use assessment to find out which children don't know their colours and target them. If the focus of your activity is to teach the children the colour 'red' then you want them to remember what you did. It needs to be fun and it needs to be exciting. While the activity is taking place you are going to take lots of photographs and these photographs will be key to your display. Not only have the key children got the motivation of seeing themselves in the display, they have also got the memory of the activity, which should then prompt the recollection of the information that you were trying to get to stick between their ears in the first place!

Top Tip from ABC ✓

An interesting exercise to do is to go into your setting and walk around it on your knees looking at what you can see directly in front of you. How much of that is key learning display? Don't just stick to inside, apply the same principle to the outdoor area (although remember your knee pads if you draw the short straw and have to do your knee walk outdoors!). I'm sure you are getting the idea by now that display should be used to raise children's self esteem and as a teaching tool.

"There's waves in the sea. Its (the boat) is crashing into them. CRASH!"

Of course these activities, although aimed at key groups of children, should never be exclusive. When your G+T pupil walks over to the 'recognising and naming red' activity and asks if they can have a go, you don't say 'Go away dear, if you look on the carousel, your group are two weeks next Tuesday! Besides which have you not got some guided reading to do?' The world does not just come in one shade of red, or green, or yellow – there are many. So when you are teaching children to recognise a colour you should have more than one shade of it for them to see. For the children who haven't got 'red' yet you might just talk about them as different reds. You might move on to dark red and light red. But when your G+T want a turn (and let's face it, they probably knew the full colour pallet whilst still in the womb) you might explain to them about the different names for the different shades and get them to name and choose their favourite. You would then have their picture in your red display as well, but their label wouldn't say 'I chose red' it would say 'I chose scarlet, or burgundy or ruby…'

Anyone looking at that display can then clearly see learning, fun and differentiation.

Top Tip from ABC

One excellent way of enhancing display and making effective use of children's voices in your environment is to put the speech into the display. So, if the children are doing a particular activity and you have photographs of them and the creation they produced as a result, add their speech too. Lots of the children will not be able to read what you have written but can tell them that what they say is really important so it gets to go on the board for everyone to read.

Speech bubbles and captions

We are forever listening out for that moment when children demonstrate their knowledge and understanding through speech. When someone says something of importance we go into a 'post-it frenzy'. We have all been in that situation when you are working with a group of children outdoors and Jazvinder announces that not only has an octopus got eight legs, it has also got tentacles! Tentacles – I ask you! What a genius! Now you feel an unstoppable urge to write that down – but oh, no! You have run out of post-its. You will have to leg it inside to get some more. By the time you get back, your focus group has disappeared and you've only just got time to scribble the relevant information on your post-it before you have to round up the next lot.

This post-it will now sit in half a plastic wallet that has been stapled to the wall under a photo of Jazvinder. This is where all of his post-its go. They live there until the next holiday when you have the laborious task of tipping each one out and then sticking it in a learning journey. Only it's so long ago that you can't really remember what happened and you were so rushed that you can't really read what you wrote. Just before you scrumple it up and throw it in the bin, you will, just for a split second, wonder what on earth you were doing that caused you to write 'testicles' on a post-it note!

Displaying what the children said during the activity gives it a whole other dimension to anyone who wasn't there at the time. This is really useful for other members of your team, senior leaders, parents and even Ofsted inspectors!

You can take this approach one step further by adding, alongside the speech bubbles, occasional 'thought clouds' where the adult can record their thoughts about what they saw and where they intend to take the learning in terms of next steps. These 'adult' statements, although invaluable, should not be invasive or dominate the display but should compliment it.

Rather than replicate all the information you use in the display in the children's learning journeys, I encourage staff to either mark a space in the learning journey where the work is going to go once the display comes down (you could use a post-it!). Photograph the relevant section of the display and stick that in or do a double copy of things like the speech bubbles before they go up.

For the first few weeks of the year in any EYFS setting you are settling children in, teaching them the rules and routines of your setting, assessing what you see (NOT hauling them off to the cloakroom to look at some sheets on a clip board) and planning to consolidate their skills and take them forward.

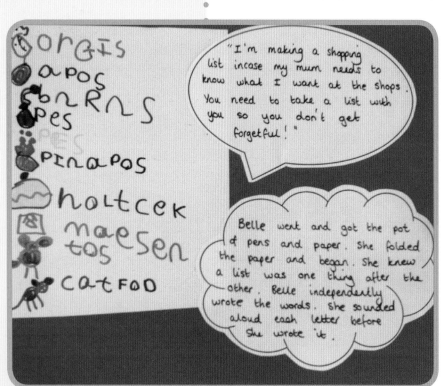

Learning stories

The first few weeks of the year is the perfect time to create your teaching displays, when you are aiming for high level engagement and personalising the environment. Not only does it raise children's interest in key areas of learning but it can also have a very positive impact on the transition into your space and within a very short time it begins to become very much their space and all of those beige walls suddenly find themselves bathed in exciting display.

As the year progresses and the children become more independent in their use of the environment and more able to lead their learning, you can use examples of their own personal learning stories to show attainment and also to interest and inspire other children.

This learning story was inspired by one question in small world play with creepy crawlies. One child asked 'Do scorpions drink water?'. The group were unable to answer the question using the knowledge in their heads but one child suggested that the internet was the answer. They looked up scorpions on the internet and then used what they found out to create a scorpion habitat. Their teacher presented the process in the style of a non-fiction text which was a format that the boys and other target children really enjoyed.

The outline, the photos and the conclusion give a crystal clear picture of how children were able to lead their own learning, succeeded in taking it forward and the role the adult played in that process. Not only does it look good, it also shows attainment and engagement.

When I am looking for truly engaging display in EYFS, and by that I don't mean the 'jaw drop' where children come in to find a rocket in the corner of the classroom and they are giddy until they have been in it twice and then they don't know what else to do with it! I mean display that shows a focus on teaching children skillls and process that they can then go on to apply in other contexts. I am looking for difference.

The days of every child doing exactly the same thing on a production line are long gone. As adults we should be teaching children how to join and stick and cut and fold, not how to make a ladybird out of a paper plate where every child has the same shape, the same colour (selected by an adult) the same legs (selected by an adult) the same spots (selected by an adult) and then 'helped' to put it all together (some more than others, by an adult!).

Apart from the fact that ladybirds are not all the shape of a paper plate and not all 'ready-mix' red. This sort of approach does nothing for engagement and is not about teaching process and everything about end result. What was the outcome of that activity? If it was that every child, regardless of their skill level or interest, had to produce a red paper plate ladybird then I would be asking why? Where is the skill? Is every child at exactly the same stage in their development? Is that stage so basic that the adult has to select every element of the activity and instruct the child how to do it? Surely the answer to those questions is never 'yes'. Then why do we do it?

In terms of engagement, if I am outside on the climbing frame having a whale of a time and you call me in because my name is next on your ladybird tick sheet and I don't want to come so you have to have stern words with me. Then I say I don't want to do a ladybird, so you have to have more stern words with me! Then I rush it because I want to get outside and I don't want to do a ladybird and you have to grip my hand and 'help' me to fill in the black bits. Then I run off as fast as I can only to find that when the ladybirds are up on the wall I don't know which one is mine because after I had gone you stuck on a couple of extra legs and a couple of extra spots! Can someone please tell me what was the point? What did I learn about anything, other than when you call me in 'to do a special job' it's going to be rubbish!

Identify the skill that you need to teach to the children *not* the activity and then let them practise and apply that skill in a way that is interesting and motivating to them. If you want to introduce me to pastels and I want to draw The Hulk – then let me! Don't force me to do daffodils just because they will look nice on your Spring display! You should be displaying what the children create with the skills you have taught them, NOT giving them an activity to create a nice display!

A scrap book display - The Gruffalo

I have been working with a few settings on a fairly regular basis for some time now and developing an approach to display that makes engagement and attainment very obvious. The concept is that they capture moments in time and show how an idea based on children's interests has grown into a full blown topic or theme.

When you have finished, the wall should look like a huge scrap book page and reflect diversity, differentiation, attainment, next steps judgements and most of all high level learning.

When I last visited The Friars Primary in Salford they had gone all 'Gruffalo'. Lots of the children in the setting were struggling with very basic aspects of PSE, especially when it came to making and maintaining friendships. The children had shown a high level of interest and enjoyment in the story of the Gruffalo, so this was used as the starting point for a mini theme.

The Gruffalo

The Mouse has got lots of friends in the wood but the Gruffalo ran away and has none, so the children decided to make him a house that he could live in. They wrote him letters to tell him all about it. To show how important the children's writing is, it has been pegged to the outside of the tent. The yellow post-its are annotations from the team. The children think that they are the staff writing to the Gruffalo to tell them how hard each child worked on their writing. That way no child thinks that they haven't done 'proper writing'!

Gregory, shows some lovely symbolic shape making in his letter, and provides a fantastic idea for an activity that will build on the theme and also impact on the development of fine and gross motor skills.

This is where daily planning can really make the difference. At the end of this session, the children might read out their letters to everyone else. When Gregory mentions his 'crocodile bread' it is the perfect opportunity to suggest bread making/ salt dough modelling for everyone. Who's idea was the activity? Who was the inspiration? Gregory! Therefore the buy-in from him and the other children is likely to be greater.

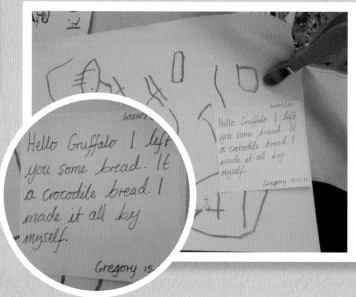

Back to the scrap book display...

Emma and her team started theirs in the top left hand corner of their main display board.

There is a photo of the main stimulus and then one of the first activities that was done in response to the interest. Now then, what we have to be really careful of is not to over theme our activities and keep thinking of the mantra 'process not end result'. In this case most children were showing high level interest in the Gruffalo. The dough was on the dough table and the dough was brown...but, what was the learning outcome attached to the dough activity? It was to develop fine motor manipulation not to make a Gruffalo. If I want to make Spiderman out of my dough and you make me make the Gruffalo then my level of engagement and involvement is going to be low. You have to be clear about why you are doing the activities you are doing and how they relate to teaching children about a process or skill rather than to produce 30 items all the same.

We used the dough to make our own Gruffalo.

Emma's setting has large and small 'scrap book' displays dotted all over it. Although they are all very different in content, and often appearance, there are a few elements that remain the same which means they are very easy to understand.

Adult explanation and context is always on green, children's speech is always in a speech bubble. This is how it looked on the Gruffalo

The addition of the adult context and the speech bubble add a huge amount of meaning to the display. The children cannot read what has been written by the adult but they know that their work was SO good that not only is it on the wall but what they said has been written down and is up there too for all to see, which has to be good for self esteem.

At the bottom left corner of the board there is a lovely collection of posters made by the children. Again the use of the speech bubbles adds context and extra depth to what might be just a 'nice' picture.

One of the children asked what would happen if the Gruffalo came to school when it was shut. Then he wouldn't be able to get into his house. This question was then thrown open to the children for discussion. Another of the children came up with the idea that they needed a house in the outdoor area, so this formed the basis of another activity and a much smaller 'scrap book' display on the window next to the outdoor area.

Remember that I said that PSE was an issue in this setting? Notice how the team have chosen photographs and quotes from the children which are positively promoting the art of being a good friend!

Here are another couple of examples of mini scrap book displays. Lots of them are on windows and doors around the setting which explains why they look a bit transparent!

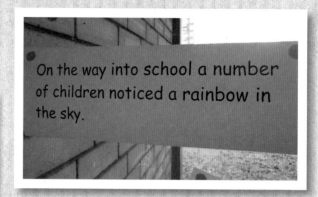

On the way into school a number of children noticed a rainbow in the sky.

Adam wanted to make a rainbow on the floor. We found some empty paint bottles and filled them with water. It was fun to squirt the paint on the ground. We used the puddles to mix new colours.

Good to see such a large group of boys colour mixing and mark making.

This green one is too hard kyle... you need to use two hands to squeeze all the green out

It's important when you create a scrap book display that you give the pieces of work room to 'breath'. If you cram a board full of 'stuff' then it begins to loose its purpose and impact.

Colour mixing, peer tutoring, being a good friend... without the speech bubble it's just two boys playing in a puddle.

Another setting I am working with are using their scrap book displays as an alternative to a learning wall. They have introduced an arrow to show where the interest started and then when it changed.

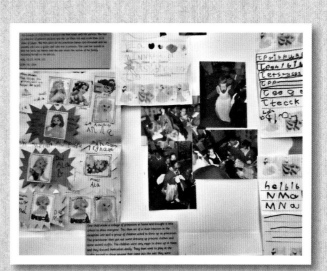

With this method, you start at one end of your board and as you work your way to the other end you identify points where children's interest changed the learning focus. Once you reach the end of your board then you just start again! Parts of the board will be constantly changing across the year. The work that you take down, you send home, file or add to individual learning journeys.

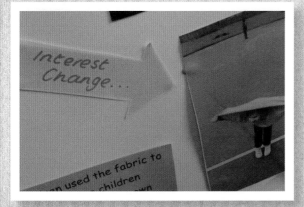

In this setting we have even used display to identify interests for more focussed learning and teaching. There are two Reception classes here who share one large space. Each morning they gather as a class to celebrate their 'uniqueness'. These are not focussed teaching sessions and the children are encourage to talk about their interests and what is going on in their lives at that time.

Outside each of the carpet spaces we have introduced an interest board. The purpose of this board is to display comments from the children, any work they have produced in school, which reflects a current interest, or anything that they bring in from home.

All of the children are encouraged to look at the interest boards on a daily basis. The things that are posted up there that cause the most interest and discussion amongst the other children are used to shape the overall theme of their learning.

The staff have annotated some of the items (in green) which allows other members of staff who were not there for the group discussion to explain it to the other children. From this board came a big theme on Disney Princesses, all inspired by this piece of work that was brought in from home.

I will explore further how thoughtful planning can support this approach in the chapter on 'Planning for Engagement'.

So, we have stripped your setting bare, backed it in beige and made a plan for how we are going to fill the walls with truly engaging display. It's probably about time that we gave some thought to the furniture!

Continuous provision

Before we can plan for continuous provision, we have to make sure that the whole team is clear about what it is. Continuous provision is a term that is now part of everyday EYFS lingo but lots of people that I meet are not quite sure what exactly it is, or they think it's the term for the 'stuff' that you have out all of the time. I agree that in essence it is the 'stuff' that is the provision bit and the 'all the time' that is the continuous bit but true continuous provision is so much more than that.

My definition of continuous provision is to continue the provision for learning in the absence of an adult. If you are putting out 'holding activities' to keep children 'busy' until it is their turn to come to your activity then yes, 'stuff' will do just fine. If however you are planning on continuing the potential for learning then it needs a great deal more thought.

Always start with your assessment, as this will tell you what it is that the children need to know. It's these needs that you will plan for when you are creating your areas of provision. Your continuous provision will change continually, not just because you will enhance it to reflect the interests of the children but also because you will change it to match their developing skill levels. Some areas of your provision might need to be much bigger at the beginning of the year when the children's skills are emergent, as opposed to the end of the year when they are more finely developed.

Continuous provision should not just be restricted to indoors. You should also be providing the same opportunities for children to develop those emergent skills outdoors. There is, however, a significant difference between indoor provision and outdoor provision, although there will be common themes that run through both. One of the many things that is unique about using the outdoor environment is that it offers a larger space that allows children to be more physical in their play. It usually also provides greater scope for making a mess without someone getting OCD about some play dough on the carpet!

Therefore the skills that you want to specifically develop in the outdoor area should be a large proportion of the ones that you cannot develop indoors. If I have a water tray outside, but it has the same resources in it as my indoor tray, it is only impacting on the same skill development that my children can do with the water inside. This is NOT outdoor play – it is indoor play outside and the difference between those two statements is significant.

Your outdoor provision should offer something that is unique to outdoors often that will involve size and noise! If your continuous provision is there to maximise on learning opportunities then it not only needs to be linked to assessment but also differentiated. If I am a bright boy and I go into the bricks as part of the continuous provision that you have set up, am I likely to think to myself 'I know, today I am not going to build a tower and knock it down. Today I will construct a suspension bridge!'? The answer is no. Lots of children go into areas of continuous provision and then spend a great deal of time engaged in non-challenging low impact play.

Children like to do things that they are good at. They are often not very willing to take on a task if there is the potential to fail so they return to doing what they know they can do well and because they can do it well, they enjoy it. Whilst 'holding areas' for children can provide lots of opportunities for personal social interaction and might have a limited use for consolidating skills they are a breeding ground for boredom, misbehaviour and wasted opportunity.

Imagine I am a child in Nursery and during my two and a half hour session I have a focussed activity in a small group with an adult that lasts around 10 to 15 minutes and a focussed carpet activity where I am one of 26 children, which also lasts for around 10 to 15 minutes. For the rest of the time I am very happily playing in my unplanned continuous provision. From that two and a half hour session I might have had 30 minutes (if I'm lucky) direct impact on my skill development and attainment. Anything that I have learned in the remaining two hours is more by luck than good planning. If I do that for a whole year in Nursery and then again in Reception that's a lot of wasted potential!

The solution is to plan your continuous provision for skill development and high-level engagement.

Let's take mark making as an example:

Mark making

First, I would look at where my children are in terms of their mark making development, splitting them into groups of similar stages.

The next step is to consider what my continuous provision needs to have in it to impact on their particular stage of development and then move them forward.

At this point I would start looking at the space I have available and making sure that the needs I have identified are being catered for.

In the very simplest of terms, if I split my mark makers into 4 groups:

- **Gross motor shoulder pivoters** (pivot from the shoulder, straight arm, stiff wrist, palm grip)

- **Elbow pivoters** (use the shoulder to support, movement has shifted to the elbow, stiff wrist, palm grip)

- **Wrist pivoters** (much smaller movement in elbow, using shoulder to support, movement comes from wrist – often stage of development where palm grip begins to change)

- **Fine motor triangulators** (triangulates grip, uses fingers as pivots, wrist, elbow and shoulder act as a support)

In my mark making areas I need resources that are going to consolidate and extend each of these groups.

For children who are still showing aspects of gross motor development and who are still working on their balance and special awareness I need big spaces (ideally these are bigger than a table top) to mark make both horizontally and vertically. Have I got them? I need mark making implements that are big and easy to grasp in various textures and colours with a few skinny ones thrown in for a bit of experimentation and good measure! With all EYFS children, but particularly at this stage of development you want to develop their hand/eye coordination and low load control (the shoulders ability to support the arm). Vertical easels for mark making and painting are great for this both indoors and out.

For my elbow pivoters I need a space that is going to encourage them to move away from their big shoulder movement into using a smaller one. What might that look like? When children first begin to elbow pivot they tend to adopt a sawing motion as this is an easier movement to do. With practice this then develops into a stirring movement with the shoulder working as a support. Have I got activities that would encourage that in an appropriate space? How do you consolidate a sawing motion and turn it into stirring? Have I got a floor space big enough for those children to utilise?

Then, when I am looking at those more fine motor skills, what develops those? Peg games, threading, tracing... the list goes on.

Assesment information

You will know that you are getting somewhere when you can say that you have looked at your assessment information and have structured your areas of provision to reflect the need identified. Not only that, you have 'dressed' the resources in the specific interest of the children giving you a better chance of engaging their interests. There is only one last piece of the jigsaw left: How do you get the blighters to use it when you are not there?

This is where the art of engagement and a child-led environment comes into its own.

'Dressing' your provision

I once worked with a practitioner who emailed me to say that she had done all of the above and still the children weren't accessing the levels of provision that she had put out for them. When we unpicked it a little further, it soon became clear why!

She had indeed assessed her children's mark making ability. Assessment had told her where her gaps were. She had also carefully thought about resources that would impact on that need. For a group of boys who needed more fine motor practice she had put onto her shelves a large box of bobbins and some laces. Great! Apart from... how many boys would be trampling across your carpet area to get to the mark making area to thread bobbins? I have yet to meet a boy who wakes up and his first thought is 'I really hope it's bobbin threading today'!

Same assessment, same activity just tailored to children's interests –
high-level engagement resulting in high level potential for attainment.

But what about actually getting them to put marks on paper? How do
you differentiate that when you are not there? Simply by using children's
interests to 'dress' your resources.

Here are two boxes next to each other on a mark making shelf. They
have been themed to the interests of the current cohort. Not only is the
contents of each box different but one offers lots of intricate fine motor
activities, the other lots of more transitional gross motor activities.

In this case assessment showed that the mark making skill level could
also be determined by gender with the girls achieving greater fine
motor control.

If I am a boy who is interested in super heroes, I am far more likely to
come into the mark making area in the first place because there is a
super hero box in there. When I get in and I am faced with these two
boxes, which one am I more likely to put my hand into?

By the same token if I am a princess loving girl who is also a nifty mark maker,
which box am I likely to put my hand into? When I do I am going to be accessing
something that has the potential to challenge me and take me forward. Otherwise
I might have been getting the paper and the felt tips out again and drawing my
thousandth pretty picture. I do it every day. I am very good at it. I do it well and it
keeps me quiet – but does it continue the provision for my learning? No!

If your gender split does not match your skill level in such a neat way then you just
might need more than two boxes.

Top Tip from ABC

The activity is great - it's just the
engagement that is lacking. The answer
came in the form of good old Ben 10! We
printed out some contact size pictures
of Ben 10 aliens and stuck them onto the
bobbins. I then wore two bobbins around my
wrist. Neither of us mentioned them to the
children. I just 'clacked' my arm around until
someone asked; 'What's that on your arm?'
and then I casually replied 'Oh, you mean my
Omnitrix? There are loads of them over
there!' And that was it - a Ben 10 stampede!
Rather than having no boys threading we
now had lots of boys threading!

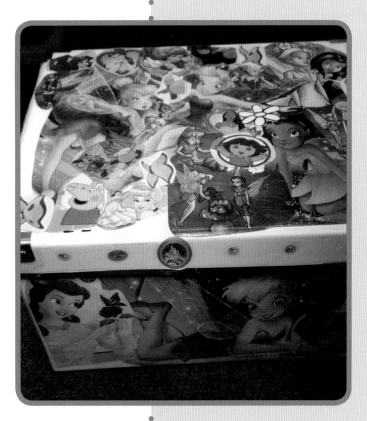

Challenge tubes

How about these old Pringles containers covered in wrapping paper or comics that reflect the interest of specific groups or individual children? Strap them onto your back and away you go – intrepid mark maker and explorer all rolled into one!

In the display section of this book I talked a great deal about how we are teaching children skills and processes rather than looking purely for an end result. This commitment to the teaching of process should be reflected in how your continuous provision is set up.

Are you sure that all of your team understand why you have workshop and art studio areas in Early Years and which skill sets they impact on? Is there provision within your setting for children to have access to a range of materials which they can self select as opposed to being given tissue paper, gummed shapes, pipe cleaners and a glue stick (as PVA is apparently far too messy for some!)?

When they arrive at the easel do they have the freedom to mix their own paint from powder as well as ready mix? Can they create any shade or do they have to use one of four colours that you have put out which will invariably lead to the scenario where someone bellows 'show me ten fingers! I can't believe I am having to say this again… but someone has put the blue brush in the red paint!'

Of course they have! Wouldn't you, if all you had to paint with was one shade of red, yellow, blue and green? When you put the red brush in the blue paint you get purple. How exciting is that? Can the children self select from a range of paper sizes, colours and textures or do they just get the off-white stuff that an adult has to fix to the easel? Bearing in mind that a lot of your children might still be at the very early stages of development and 'pivoting from their shoulder', have you created a vertical surface that is big enough to let them do that and also offer opportunities for collaborative painting, which could impact on personal social skills, as well as peer tutoring.

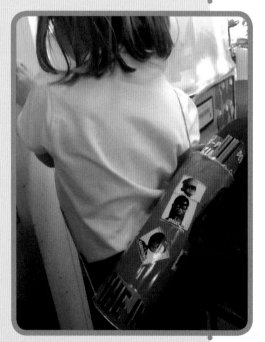

When you have taught the children to make and use thick or textured paint in their work, is it available for them to use from then on? If you teach a child a skill then you want to see them apply that skill independently. They cannot do that if textured paint was an 'event' and not a 'process'.

You get high levels of engagement in these areas when children can have a bigger choice not always about what they do but definitely how they do it.

Process NOT end result

As the school term comes to an end and the summer holidays are about to begin, the early sunflowers begin to unfurl their golden petals – a sure sign that summer is here. But do not fear, the late bloomers, the really big 'Blue Peter competition winners' will not be at their best until we return to school. This means you have not missed out on the opportunity to reach in to the back of the stock cupboard and pull out your faithful Van Gogh! Now, don't get me wrong. I like Van Gogh. If you are going to 'do' a painter he has something for everyone. Don't forget, there are some children who will visibly wilt at the sight of a vase full of yellow flowers. If you are thinking about trying to get high levels of engagement then flowers don't always do it! But, Van Gogh came up trumps due to the fact that he was a little unhinged and chopped off his own ear (now that is more like it)! Better than that he then painted a picture of himself in a rather fetching bandage…

When we look at the 'style' of an artist that is exactly what we should be teaching. What techniques did Van Gogh use that made lots of his pictures have the same feel even though the content and colours were often different? In essence for me, it comes down to 'very thick paint' and using something other than a brush - fingers, a play dough tool or a kitchen spatula.

I am sure Van Gogh didn't use a kitchen spatula but the whole point is that we don't want children to paint exactly like Van Gogh – we are looking at style. Like everything else in the EYFS it should be about teaching children a 'process' that they don't associate with just one thing but that they can creatively apply to many situations.

You should not get all of the children to produce a version of 'Sunflowers' because the learning outcome was not 'to accurately produce a copy of a great masterpiece'! By saying to children that they must all produce a version of Van Gogh's painting, you are setting them up to fail and closing down any chance of them expressing their own creativity. Instead you need to identify the technique/process and let the children experiment with it, producing any sort of picture they want to.

You shouldn't be giving children work to 'create a display' – you 'display the work' that they have 'created' using the processes you have taught them.

So… if you have sunflowers in your setting and you look at their sheer gorgeousness you might well talk to the children about this bloke who is famous for painting pictures (and cutting off his ear). I would show them his painting of sunflowers and a variety of his other work. Tell them that he used oil paints which are thick and shiny. Enthuse over the how fantastically squidgy thick shiny paint feels, especially when you apply it with your fingers! Then show the children how to add flour to ready-mix paint to really thicken it up and some PVA to make it shiny when it dries (just like oil paint). Give them the paint and the flour and the glue and let them go for it!

Your resulting display will not be thirty different versions of sunflowers by Van Gogh but paintings using thick paint inspired by the work of Van Gogh, inspired by a sunflower growing in your garden.

When we teach children a new skill we then want them to be able to apply it to a variety of situations and not think that you can only use thick paint if you are painting sunflowers with a bandage over your ear!

Top Tip from ABC

Sometimes practitioners will tell me that EYFS children are just too young or too messy to have this level of freedom around paint! Well, in my book you cannot teach process without a bit of mess and it's actually from the disasters that you learn the most. With regard to age and capability, I have worked with settings where children as young as two have successfully accessed and used all of their own creative resources – both indoors and out.

Here is a three year old in a pre-school experiencing powder paint, first as a dry texture and then with a squirt of water, as a medium for painting.

He was not required to paint with a brush on a piece of paper in one of four colours selected for him by an adult, he 'painted' with his hands onto the table top following his exploration of the powder. You could seriously see his brain cells working!

In that same setting, at the same time, a visiting adult (not me!) was talking to a little girl who was also keen to paint. The adult demonstrated how to paint a rainbow and then gave it to the child to 'finish'. So, like with any good paint by numbers she just filled in the blanks – blue sky, green grass, one tree and one flower.

When it came to the flower the girl took her painting out of the painting area to the mark making table (I was pleased, but not surprised, to see that this is not only allowed, but actively encouraged) and she drew a very beautiful flower in felt tip pen. I asked her why she had done this and she very eloquently explained that it was due to the size of brushes available, the thickness of the paint and the space on her paper where the flower 'needed to be'. This was a 3 year old who knew her way around that painting station and had experienced it in some detail. Although she was perfectly happy to 'finish off' someone else's painting you couldn't see her brain cells working. When I asked her if she was going to take it home, her reply said it all: 'No, it's not mine!'

Although 'no child sustained any long term damage in the making of this picture', it just reminded me that true creativity comes from the opportunities to really explore and experiment with a huge variety of resources where adults teach children about 'processes' and not just an end result. My general rule of thumb – it's not Blue Peter so don't have 'one you made earlier' as that tends to stifle not inspire!

Role-play

Another area of provision that has huge potential, especially in terms of children's personal, social and language development, is role-play; yet it is often very adult-led and actually has the potential to restrict engagement and learning rather than enhance it.

Children use role-play for a variety of different reasons but one of the main things they do in it is to re enact their own life in an effort to make sense of it. The key thing to remember is that you can only role-play what you know. If you know a great deal about something then you will role-play it well. If you only know a little then you can only role-play a little. What we often do as practitioners is put children in a situation where we are asking them to role-play a scenario they know very little about. How many of the children that you work with go to a restaurant regularly enough to know how it operates? How many visit the Post Office? How many have been in the operating theatre of a vet? When was the last time any of us booked our holiday at a travel agent?

We spend ages setting up our role-play areas, only to find that by the end of the first week one of us is pinned against the wall, creeping up on the unsuspecting role-players like a member of the SAS and then hissing at them 'Get out, I have told you before this is a VET not a place to play BEN 10, now go and find something else to do!' The reason they play Ben 10 is that they haven't got the knowledge or language to role-play the vet scenario or any tactics for keeping it interesting.

Considering we are trying to use this area of provision to impact on language development – we are not doing a very good job! This is where your differentiation comes in. As a team, you need to sit down and discuss why exactly you have a role-play area and the differences between an adult leading the play and introducing children to new experiences and language and children being in there during periods of continuous provision on their own and needing to rehearse, replay and consolidate what they know.

Deconstructed role-play

By far the best mechanism I have ever used to accomplish all of the above is to create a deconstructed role-play space that has a good mix between child-led and adult-initiated role-play. To run a deconstructed role-play area the children you are working with have to have spent enough time on the Earth to be familiar with lots of aspects of day to day life.

A good deconstructed role-play area needs to be big enough to get a few children in it. If you have identified language and personal skills as key for development then they need to be represented in a large portion of your environment. If your role-play is one small corner which becomes packed with three children in it, then it's unlikely to have any significant impact. You are going to fill your identified space with things that can be anything! By that I mean things like: cardboard boxes, large sheets, crates, bread trays – the list is endless.

You want to create a role-play space that can change continually depending on who is in it. A café is a café until you change it into the vet. A pile of boxes can also be a café and ten minutes later a vet and then a submarine and then my granny's house. It is this level of versatility that not only challenges children to use their imaginations but also offers high-level engagement.

It might look something like this:

It is certainly not as 'pretty' as your conventional café but the possibilities are far greater. If I am setting these up, I often take out all of the costumes and replace them with pieces of fabric – again this encourages children to really use their imagination and creativity.

Top Tip from ABC

There is also no display in my deconstructed role-play. The walls are backed in plain paper and the children are encouraged to draw a backdrop that suits their play. Don't expect them to produce something like a theatre set! You will often get a series of small drawings and marks, which the children then play to.

The role of the adult

The role of the adult in moving play forward is sometimes to play alongside children within the context of the role-play they have created, and sometimes to offer new language and experience by leading the play.

In one setting, a little girl's mum had a baby and brought him in and bathed him. This started a great deal of interest in babies so we set up a baby box in which we put all the things to do with babies, including all the books that we had been reading.

In another setting, a child's dog had puppies and the children were interested in the vet so we got the vet to come and visit and then we set up a vet's box which had all the things that we would have used in our vets role-play. When the adult went into the role-play to 'teach' they would lead the play and set up the boxes and crates to be the vet. They would use all of the language and resources to act out (as much as they knew) about being at the vet's. When the adult left the role-play the boxes stayed.

Some children might choose to carry on the vet play. Some might take some of the vet resources and use them in their own role-play which is nothing to do with the vet, and some might not use the vet resources at all and play something completely different. All of these scenarios are fine as the 'teaching' session is over and children are interpreting what they have learnt in their own way.

Often you will get two or three different role-plays happening in the same space at the same time allowing for maximum diversity. This style of role-play is perfect for outdoors as well as in.

Top Tip from ABC ✓

In response to children's interest, I would create enhancement boxes that the children could access once they had been introduced into the play. I always have a 'home' box full of the familiar items that you would normally have in your home corner. Then I would create boxes that linked to the theme we were looking at or particular children's interest.

Small world play

I often apply the same principle to small world play. A pig is a pig and a helicopter is (apart from being impossible to pronounce for most children!) a helicopter whereas a plain wooden brick, much like a cardboard box, can be anything! Often, less is more when it comes to basic provision especially when developing language and imagination is involved.

When it comes to engaging continuous provision, in lots of respects an area like mark making is a fairly simple one to start with as the progression is obvious. When you have really mastered effective continuous provision then you would be able to show how you had levelled it in and then dressed it for engagement in all areas.

You cannot guarantee what a child will do when they are in continuous provision, without an adult to guide and support them, but what you can do is know that you have maximised the *potential* for learning and minimised the *risk* of failure.

We will have a look at how you might plan for this sort of provision in the next chapter.

Planning for engagement

Throughout this book I have talked about how children are often most engaged in their learning when their learning is about them. Therefore, it makes perfect sense to me that planning should reflect this. Time and time again I have sat watching a group of Nursery children be taught about the seven main types of housing in Great Britain and wondered how it can be a valuable use of their leaning time to spend 20 minutes just trying to say the word 'bungalow'!

How relevant is your planning to the children you have got sitting in front of you? Do they have any concept of what or where Antarctica is? When you say that they 'all love our pirates topic'. Do they?

Although looking at learning through a 'topic' approach can introduce children to lots of experiences and opportunities for learning it can also stifle them through lack of interest, meaning and engagement. For me, the process of planning for all children is simply this:

Step 1 Assessment

Assessment is always your starting point as this tells you what the children can do really well and also where their areas of development are. Once you have identified your next steps in all areas of development then you know what it is that you are going to teach.

At this point in the planning process it is really important that you focus on skill, development and NOT activity. One of the biggest shifts that practitioners often have to make when they move to a personalised learning approach is to view all of the 'usual' activities as a bank of resources that they can draw upon if they are appropriate and not a definite, foregone conclusion.

I now know where the gaps are in each area of learning and I have identified 'next steps' skill development for each of those gaps.

Step 2 PLODS

At this point in the process, I would sit down with the team and do a planning session where we would come up with some **PLODS** (Possible Lines Of Development). These are practitioner's ideas for resources, events and types of activity that would provide the required learning opportunity to impact on the skill development required e.g. I might have identified that I need to further develop fine motor skills with a group of children. When I am thinking about a PLOD for this group I would be gathering together ideas of resources that would impact on this skill development. So I might list the inside and outside equipment that we have. One PLOD might be that the children use small amounts of clay to give them the experience of a new medium for modelling and also encourage fine motor movement. What I would not plan is what they are going to make out of the clay. My outcome is linked to fine motor development and therefore the children should be able to model whatever they want.

If I plan that we are all going to make a coil pot for Mother's Day, I am providing an activity that fills the skills gap identified but what I am also doing is restricting the opportunities for engagement by imposing the subject of the clay modelling. My outcome is related to fine motor development *not* the production of a coil pot. Therefore, my PLOD is 'to use clay or other malleable materials to impact on fine motor development'.

If children are uninspired and not sure what to make then you could show them a wide range of possibilities for inspiration or spend some time asking open questions to help define an outcome.

Picture the scene: In the middle of a table there is a spectacular arrangement of Primulas (the spring flower not the processed cheese!). Around the flowers are some beautifully sliced A5 sheets of sugar paper in lemon, powder blue, lilac and pink. Also on the table there are two pots. One is filled with chalk and the other with oil pastels. In both pots there are only the colours of the flowers and green.

The practitioner leading the activity is currently producing a masterpiece of her own on a pink piece of paper which she will then use as a teaching tool. The important thing to know about this activity is that the planned focus was 'To introduce the children to the use of chalk and oil pastels'. It was not 'to produce an accurate observational drawing of a Primula'.

Top Tip from ABC

At this stage in the planning process, your mantra has to be 'process not activity'. Keep asking the question 'What is the outcome/objective of this activity?' Is it to develop a skill or is it so that all children regardless of their interests or ability will produce a similar version of the same thing?

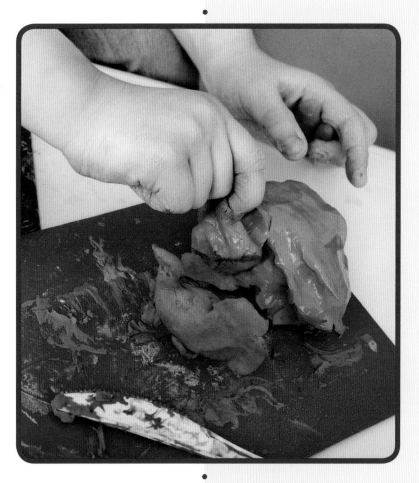

There was no getting away from the fact that this activity had been colour coordinated within an inch of it's life and looked very pretty (to an adult). When I looked at it, I was thinking of my own three boys, and many like them, who at this age would have given the table a wide berth purely because it had pink and flowers on it! These would have been the boys that you were dragging in from the outside area who would then give you minimum engagement, minimum effort and then get minimum outcomes.

My first question to the practitioner was 'If I came to this table, could I draw The Hulk?' to which the response was 'No, because we are doing spring flowers'. When I queried what the planned objective was I then asked again if I could draw The Hulk. There was a VERY stony silence before I was told 'that in theory, yes, but I want the children to do spring flowers.'

I completely get the fact that you might want to introduce a skill through a subject that is linked to another area of learning, but in that case you have really got to think about all of your children and how engaged they would be by, in this case, spring flowers. But, in this instance that wasn't the plan. This was just about chalk and pastels.

Never one to take a hint, I then asked if I could draw my Hulk on some different paper, to which I got the response. Through gritted teeth, 'No!' When I politely enquired why not, I was told that sugar paper is the best thing for pastels and chalk. Now, apart from the fact that that this isn't true, good EYFS practice should be about teaching process, letting children experiment and find out with a wide range of resources to choose from. If the activity is to introduce the children to pastels and chalk, then you could spend a few minutes on the carpet with everyone showing them what pastels and chalk are and generally making them sound like the most amazing thing that has ever been invented. Then you would let your children know where they could access them with a variety of other resources and let them experiment and produce what they were engaged by.

There is nothing to stop you from having your Primulas out in your setting as you will have been investigating them in relation to the advent of spring but you certainly wouldn't be asking everyone to draw them. Then you would display what the children produced in relation to the use of pastels and chalk as opposed to producing a spring display where everyone had drawn Primulas!

Top Tip from ABC

When you are thinking about your PLODS then you will also plan in teaching around any events, festivals, seasons, celebrations etc that will be experienced by all of the children. You know that in Autumn term you will have planning around events such as bonfire night and Christmas. In the new year you will be looking at seasons and growth. None of that changes, it is just how you present it to the children that will make the difference.

Step 3   Responding to children's interests

I think it's a really good idea to get children's interests up on display. It often engenders great discussions amongst them but also shows how you are using their interest to inform your planning. There are lots of ways to do it.

Now that you have got your next steps identified, a collection of solutions created by practitioners based on their knowledge of skill development and resources available, and children have identified their areas of high level interest – you can get going. Child-led learning does NOT just mean asking the children what they fancy getting out today and then doing that! Young children can only select from the experiences that they have had so far in their lives. If you have only ever asked a child to choose what they would like to do then they wouldn't be able to expand that selection very much.

Part of our role is to give children new experiences, things that they don't even know that they don't know! The secret is how we deliver those experiences. When they are part of something the children enjoy and they think it was their idea in the first place – that is when you usually get maximum impact.

Top Tip from ABC

Once you have identified your next steps and your PLODS, then this is where you begin to focus on planning for engagement based on children's interests. The best way to find out what the children are interested in is just to listen to what they are talking about. I tend to find that if you sit them in a circle and ask them they either make it up, don't know or say the same as everyone else. If your environment and practice includes lots of opportunities for talk you will end up with plenty to go on.

Chapter 6

Engagement through creativity: Case studies

The EYFS (2012) describes Creativity as:

> *Children have and develop their own ideas, make links between ideas, and develop strategies for doing things.*

It's often not the opportunities to express and communicate these ideas that are lacking but the frequency and variety of these opportunities that makes children's creativity attainment difficult to judge. Children need lots of opportunities to:

- **Explore media and materials**

- **Create music and dance**

- **Develop imagination and imaginative play**

True creativity is about *taking risks* and making connections and is *strongly linked to play*.

The key to providing a high level creativity opportunity is that:

Children's responses to what they see, hear and experience through their senses are individual and the way they represent their experiences is unique and valuable.

The two sentiments that should really stand out in the above statement are *individuality* and *uniqueness*. How can you express your individuality and uniqueness if you are on a production line to make a paper plate ladybird or a kitchen roll penguin? To allow creativity to flourish and provide lots of opportunities for assessment, we need to teach children skills and processes and not always start with the end result. No longer should we see the whole group making the same thing or the practitioner showing their finished example before the children have started. We show children how to… join, how to… use chalk, how to… mix thick paint.

How they use that skill should be up to them and led by their imaginations, not dictated by us! We then display what the children create. The remit of this project was to work with four schools who had already started their journey down the path of 'creativity enlightenment' and just give them a few ideas to help them along the way.

After our initial meeting we planned a 'Creativity focus' to meet that settings particular needs.

Case study 1

Project: **CS1**

Setting: Reception class in a primary school

The brief:

This school is in an area that has pockets of significant challenge and the children tend to arrive well below the expected level for their age in the majority of areas. This year's intake are particularly poor in talk, speech, listening and PSE – especially sharing. Add to that the fact that there are 23 boys – yes, I will say it again 23 BOYS and 7 girls… you get the picture!

The teacher and TA have their work cut out – but are clearly up for the challenge! What excited me most about my visit that day was the fact the ladies had decided to ditch the old 'Autumn' or 'Ourselves' usual September 'topic' approach and go with a theme inspired by the children's interests - being detectives!

As a result the children walked into a crime scene! Lightening McQueen was planning a party and **someone** had put mud all over the wheeled toys making them filthy. Who could it have been?

Well, what clues would you look for? If you had been smearing things with mud how might you look? That was it – dirty hands! So the hunt for dirty hands began.

Then the culprit was found… Charlie! Check out those hands!

Next challenge… to get those bikes cleaned up by building a car wash. The children did a brilliant building job. There was so much learning involved in it.

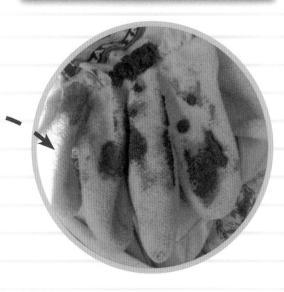

Part of the children's design was that there were gaps in the roof to let the water through and the walls were re-built so that they had gaps to squirt the water through just like a 'real' car wash!

Very quickly the bikes were washed and washed and washed again. There were lots of opportunities for large and small scale mark making – signs were soon made to tell customers when the car wash was open and closed.

A health and safety check was even carried out by non other than Bob the Builder himself (or so he said)!

Whilst all this was happening there were lots of other pockets of high level engagement all over the setting. It was clear to see that activities had been specifically planned to develop those emergent skills.

This was a good one for gross motor, fine motor, hand/eye coordination and balance (and mud)!

Much of our afternoon was spent discussing how the curriculum needed to be carefully structured to reflect the genetic make up of the group, making sure that the girls didn't miss out because of the 'boyness' of lots of the boys. Also that the environment and planning that was taking place needed to respond to the immediate and fundamental needs of this particular cohort. In the short term, this might mean not giving the full and broad access to the EYFS curriculum that you would ideally like – but on the other hand there is no point in trying to give the children everything if they don't have the skills to access the learning or use the environment correctly.

When practitioners are observing and assessing they are then recording children's attainment against the next steps that they had planned in each area of learning. When it comes to subsequent planning they are just looking for consolidation or next steps.

Once again you plan the objective or outcome as opposed to the activity and then 'dress' that objective in the interests of the children.

The cycle of planning just keeps moving forward in this way.

Case study 2

Project: **Fairy folk**

Setting: A three-form entry primary school with its own nursery.

The brief:

The staff had had lots of success with individual topics and themes such as 'aliens'. Their feeling was that although the children had got a great deal out of them they occurred in short bursts and were very specific. They wanted to create a creativity theme that was constant and that they could dip in and out of, giving it more or less focus depending on the other demands of the curriculum.

The result of our thinking was **PROJECT FAIRY FOLK!**

How it worked

I was going to be introduced to the children as a 'fairy folk finder' whose job it was to travel around the country and track down communities of fairies. I agreed to dress up and go into the school and have a session with each of the classes, convincing them, that I worked for the government and showing them lots of evidence (it's amazing what you can get from Google images these days!). You can find a copy of the Powerpoint I used here (abcdoes.com). We wanted the children to see the fairies as a community that lived and worked in the EYFS outdoor area. We were clear that these were not Disney, Tinkerbell fairies but very much the original folk law 'little people'. We didn't ever show any of the children close up images of the fairies as we wanted them to use their imaginations.

At this point you can let your imagination run wild! Sometimes the adults created scenarios for the children about things that the fairies needed or wanted and lots of the time the children just came up with them themselves. Don't be fooled by thinking this is 'one for the girls'. Far from it, the boys really took to the idea. Because these fairies live and work like we do you can ask the children to help with all sorts of tasks from recording music for a fairy party to constructing a bridge to get across a puddle or making a shelter that is waterproof.

The staff purchased doll's house crockery and cutlery to leave for discovery outdoors. The children also found a tiny hat (blown off in the wind) and a tiny boot (stuck in a muddy puddle). The fairies were not always there. This allowed staff to keep the project fresh by out of the blue leaving a sign or a request from the fairy folk.

The fairies left various gifts and objects for the children and in return the children made things (to scale) for the fairies and left them out for them. One fairy even visited the classroom overnight and left fairy footprints for the children to discover! The staff used talk boxes to encourage the children to record their songs and music for fairy parties. These were left outside stuck into 'fairy dance houses' made in the outdoor workshop.

Some children produced a fairy newspaper with school news in it, others fashioned clothes, cards and pets from tiny bits of card, paper and fabric. It was easily possible to cover all of the creativity profile points through considered use of this stimulus.

Of course, this project wasn't limited to creativity, it had a huge impact on the children's independent activity choices, especially in relation to mark making. And do you know what? Rumour has it that the fairies are still living there to this day, but that doesn't mean to say you haven't got another group living in your outdoor area. Make sure you keep a sharp eye out!

Reflections from the team

Alistair came into school to introduce the fairy folk within our EYFS setting. The project was really positive. It improved the children's creative development, particularly developing their imagination skills, especially within Reception. We also found that some of the quieter children within the setting became more confident and engaged within the activities. It inspired lots of communication and became a topic that the children referred back to throughout the rest of the year. As teachers we really enjoyed the theme and liked the fact that it could be an on-going thread for the children that were really captured by it.

Case study 3

Project: Outdoor space

Setting: A two-form entry primary school

The brief:

This school's Reception classes have access to an outdoor space that is enclosed on three sides by other parts of the school building. The side that is not enclosed is built in such a way that it creates a substantial 'wind tunnel' effect whenever there is so much as even a light breeze! Due to the position of the space in relation to the buildings around it, there is only one small corner that gets direct sunlight. This means that on occasion the space is dull, windy and cold.

It is little wonder then that some children are reluctant to play out in it. The school had invested funding to enhance the existing space and purchased a wooden play house, a sand pit on legs, three wooden planters, a covered area and some playground markings.

Whilst confident that they were offering lots of opportunities for children to explore the aspects of creativity indoors, the Reception team felt that they wanted to focus on the outdoor space, the equipment they put in it and also how they could plan their outdoor play to encourage a creative approach to learning.

How it worked

Our first task was to look at the space and work out its potential. There was some funding available for the purchase of resources but much of the work would have to be done on a minimum budget. Creativity was required all round!

I observed the children at play in the existing space and looked at what they accessed and what they didn't. I then asked the children about their favourite places to play outside and their least favourite places to play. Their answers were very enlightening e.g. even though there was a wooden play house in the corner they didn't like playing in it because it was damp and had spiders and the wind blew through the windows (the wind was a recurring theme!).

Once we had identified the potential in what was already available, we made some decisions about the sort of play we wanted to encourage in that space. We decided we would like to create:

- **Lots more mark making opportunities**
- **Space to grow plants**
- **Large scale construction**
- **Large scale water play**
- **Large scale sand area**
- **Exploratory tray**
- **Den making area**
- **Small world habitats**
- **A more challenging track**

Mark making opportunities

At the beginning of the project the provision for mark making was under the covered veranda. It consisted of a table and chairs and a trolley full of mark making materials. This was occasionally used by the children but due to its position, the contents of the tray was often to be found blowing around the area!

We decided to increase the number of mark making areas by introducing a number of child height blackboards. These were easily made from exterior ply that had been painted with blackboard paint. We also reused the existing white board and extended the provision further by introducing Perspex as a new mark making surface. (As part of the 'damp' play house makeover the windows were covered in Perspex sheeting. This not only kept out the breeze and rain but allowed the children to paint on the Perspex from both inside and out.) We also made the decision to extend the mark making opportunities beyond the original space and put large blackboards on the wall near the track and main play space.

Space to grow plants

The setting already had a number of tyres dotted around the outdoor space that were filled with soil and seasonal flowers. In an effort to 'soften' some of the hard bare walls we fixed lengths of guttering to the wall at child height. These 'growing gutters' were then filled with compost and planted with seeds and plants with shallow roots. The existing wooden planters were over grown with shrubs (some dead)! These were going to be dug out, leaving minimum planting. More about that later.

Large scale construction

I wanted the children to have the opportunity to build on a large scale and also to build with construction materials that could be used in a variety of different ways thereby encouraging their creative thought processes. We moved the 'community play blocks' to a central space and then enhanced them with large cardboard tubes and boxes.

Large scale water play

The children already had access to an outdoor tap which they managed themselves very successfully. We just needed to take the practice that was already in place and extend it further. To give the water play another dimension, we fixed lengths of guttering to an outside wall. The guttering was fixed at an angle to allow the water to 'waterfall' down the wall. There were endless possibilities for helping or hindering the flow of water. Of course you are not restricted only to the use of water! You can use gloop, slime, wallpaper paste – anything fluid. If you didn't want to use this space just for water play then you could also use balls of various sizes, shapes and types to test in your guttering.

Large scale sand/exploratory play

Although the existing sand tray was a really good size, it was also very tall and the children had to stand on a milk crate to reach into it. This resulted in lots of sand on the floor and not a great deal in the tray. The plan was to chop the legs off the sand tray and turn it into an investigation/exploration tray which would have various different contents for the children to play in/with.

The biggest planned transformation was for the outdoor play house. The plan was to cover the large open windows with Perspex (as previously mentioned), block up one third of the door height (creating a step in from the outside) and fill with two feet of sand. Thereby creating an all-weather indoor sand pit where children could take off their shoes and socks and also actually dig rather than just play.

Sand play resources were stored in baskets that were hung from hooks around the walls of the 'sand house' leaving the whole floor area clear. By the end of my time with the project, the Perspex was in place and the original sand tray had significantly shorter legs! Project 'sand house' was just about to begin.

Den making area/Small world habitats

Once again we tried to be as creative as we could with the space that we had. The three existing wooden planters were connected by two bench seats. Observations had shown that the children rarely used this area for sitting in and showed little interest in what was growing in the planters.

I felt that as the children were not making use of the outdoor play house that they needed somewhere to explore role-play outdoors as well as having the opportunity to build and create a shelter.

We decided to turn the planter area into a den making space. All this took was the addition of some wooden poles to the sides of the planters and three lengths of camping washing line. Add to that a large basket of fabric and that is that!

The children can access this activity independently and very quickly create their own unique spaces to play. It's often difficult to differentiate between your small world play outdoors and indoors. One of the biggest things that you can do to enhance outdoor small world play is to create 'real' habitats. Grass for the park, jungles for tigers, mud pools for elephants etc. The wooden planters were perfect for creating three very different habitats. Some with existing planting and others where all/some of the original planting had been replaced with textured materials such as bark, sand, stones, soil. As children made dens using the interior of the space, others could create small world habitats on the exterior.

A more challenging track

There was this track, these boys and these bikes… all they wanted to do was ride round and round and round and round so one day…

This is a scenario that is not unique but was a particular issue. The solution that we came up with was to create regular 'track challenges' e.g. 'a volcano has erupted in the middle of your track! Can you use the blocks to build a bridge over it?' 'We have decided that you now have to pay to go around our track. Can you build a bridge where you can stop drivers and collect their money?'

The idea is to try and incorporate as many of the other features of the outdoors as possible in the challenges, especially the mark making.

Reflections from the team

Although the children already enjoyed using our outdoor area we faced a number of challenges for Alistair to address:

- The outdoor area is a 'quad' area which acts as a thoroughfare for children and staff to get to other areas of the school.

- The quad creates a 'wind tunnel' effect and is shaded from the sun (and any potential warmth) for most of the year.

- The equipment has to be brought in and out every morning and evening to prevent overnight 'tampering'.

- We had some distinct areas of learning and needed to add more.

- We had some 'practical' problems accessing some of the equipment.

Alistair experienced the full hospitality of Blackpool weather on his visits and was regularly drenched or blown away by the wind.

- He suggested a low budget way to create a wind barrier by tying bamboo cane to the railings. This was a cheap effective solution and also aesthetically pleasing. He didn't manage to stop it raining though!

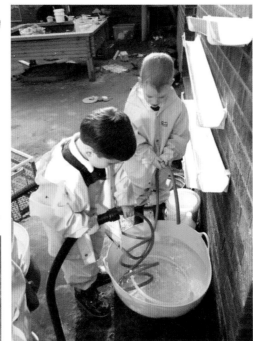

Alistair solved some of our practical problems:

- He suggested sawing the legs off our sandpit so that the children could reach inside without standing on blocks (Why didn't we think of that? Sometimes you just need a fresh pair of eyes!).

- He provided low cost storage solutions for our pens and writing equipment by suggesting we use drainpipes which can be clipped on and off brackets.

- He suggested minimising the wind whistling through our role-play house by adding Perspex to the window spaces – this could also be used for mark making.

- Alistair helped us to develop creativity in particular:

- Water play – again a 'cheap but effective' solution to create a 'drainpipe' water fall by adding lots of brackets onto a wall.

- Den making – three raised flower beds were used as the foundation for a new den making area. Wooden poles and camping wire have been attached so that the children can add their own materials and create their own dens. Alistair's real challenge came when the water play flooded the new den area – solved with support from our site supervisor.

Case study 3

Project: **Bones**

Setting: Moor Park - a two-form entry primary school with a nursery.

The brief:

This time our creativity project had a 'boy' focus. Moor Park were exploring possible solutions to the common issue of engaging boys in the more creative aspects of continuous provision. What the team were finding was that when there was an adult present in a 'creative' area then (with persuasion) more boys would visit. When there was no adult present, lots of boys would avoid these areas favouring others such as outdoor or construction. The challenge was to create an activity that would engage the boys and encourage them to access all areas of creativity during continuous provision – no mean feat!!

How it worked

I based the project around the discovery of bones in the outdoor area. The children were going to discover these bones and then they would be set a 'video challenge'. They would be given a minute timer and a Flip video camera. The challenge was to make a minute video about the bones.

There were only two rules:
1) that the video had to be no longer than one minute
2) that the bones were the only 'real' objects that could be used. Anything else had to be made. So, if you wanted music in your video… make it. A truck? Make it. Scenary? Make it! You get the picture.

The videos would be shown occasionally at the end of the day to maintain momentum and best practice identified to help the children to understand the expectation.

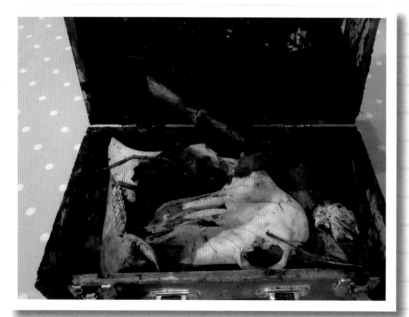

The digging up of the bones caused great excitement. Immediately the children decided that they belonged to a dinosaur. The children understood the task and found using the video cameras very easy. One thing they were not so good at was stopping after a minute so some of their videos did go on a bit! There were lots of nice surprises that came out of the project, especially with regard to mark making. One boy even created a newsletter to tell parents about the gruesome discovery (see photos).

The staff made floor books to record the progress of the project. The inclusion of the children's thoughts, questions and speech gave the book a real context and relevance (see photos). After initially starting the project I visited some weeks later to see how it had progressed. There had been huge initial interest in the bones and the children had produced some great work both on paper and using the video.

Staff reported that the interest in the bones then dwindled to just a few hard core palaeontologists! However the children started using the video cameras in different parts of the setting, even documenting the capture of a frog and its eventual release into the school pond.

On my final visit to the setting I took in a pop corn making machine and the children made their own popcorn and we 'officially' watched the product of all of their hard work. It was not quite the Cannes Film Festival – but it was close!

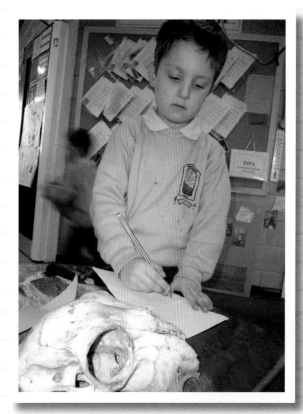

Reflections from the team

When Alistair came in to observe our environment, he noticed that the boys were engaged in 'typical' activities such as building with the wooden bricks or having their tea made for them by the girls in the role-play area! Very few were painting, drawing or writing. We decided that our focus for the project would be to engage boys in creativity, particularly outside, along with teaching the children how to use the flip videos to record their own 'movies'.

Bones!

Alistair left us a box of bones to bury outside. The discovery of them led to:

- Lots of discussion about what they were and where they had come from

- Writing letters, labels and signs

- Drawing the bones after looking at them through magnifiers

- Making one minute movies using the flip video cameras

- Making a large scrap book of photos and writing for parents to see

- Language development and questioning

All of which was led by the boys!

Cinema day

The children soon became used to using the Flip cameras although the majority of their movies were over one minute long. They were filming dens being built, frogs found outside - anything! They then created their own cinema (a few times) which involved:

- Numbering seats and making tickets

- Making pop corn and boxes suitable to hold it

- Making signs and lists of favourite films

- Making the props for the movies

- Organising the staff! The camera man, the ticket sellers, popcorn man and the actors

- Language development and questioning

This inspired both the girls and the boys and it was great to see them working together.

Alistair returned to watch the movies made by the children and to make the all important pop corn!

Since the creativity project we have also introduced a deconstructed role-play area as suggested by Alistair. We were very cynical at first but the results have been fantastic. The children are very creative with the selection of boxes and tubes and have played with them much more effectively than they ever did in the 'home corner'. We really enjoyed the creativity project and since Alistair's visits we saw a real change in the boys and their attitude towards creative activities. They were definitely inspired and so were we.

Case study 5

Project: **Deconstructed role-play**

Setting: A two-form entry primary school with a nursery.

The brief:

Both Reception classes at this setting shared the same large space and therefore had equal access to the provision. The team had identified that an area for improvement was the children's creative play in the indoor role-play area. Many of the children lacked a varied range of expressive and descriptive language and would often resort to familiar and non-challenging role-play. By 'deconstructing' the current role-play area, our aim was to encourage children to move away from the scaffolding of the familiar play equipment and create play scenarios of their own.

How it worked

At the beginning of the project, the role-play area was set up as a home corner with wooden house furniture and the usual household items as props. There was a selection of dressing up clothes and character costumes. We removed all of the house furniture from the space leaving only open shelving. Any character costumes were also removed. We set up a separate role-play area as part of the reading area so that children could use the character costumes to help to develop their language for story and familiar role-play.

The role-play area was then stripped of any posters, digital images and coloured backing. The walls were covered in cream lining paper to create spaces for mark making. Camping washing lines were suspended between the shelving and the walls and also across the corners of the space to allow children to create their own den/play space if they wanted to.

Any themed resources such as house or shop were collected together and put into storage boxes/baskets that would be kept on the open shelving. Children could then decide to create a café or a vet if that was what they were interested in but they were not tied to one role-play theme until the adult decided to change it. The costumes were replaced with large and small pieces of fabric that would encourage children to think creatively about how they were going to use these pieces of material for dressing up or den making. If a child is wearing a Snow White costume then they can be nobody else but Snow White, whereas a piece of fabric could be hundreds of different characters.

The last addition to the deconstructed role-play was a collection of large cardboard boxes. Following the project the team would add to these with a variety of objects that could be anything i.e. small boxes, crates, rubber tubes and cardboard lids etc. After being used to their play being dictated for them, the children sometimes needed to observe modelling from an adult or other children. Once they became familiar with the expectation, their play became dramatically more unique, personal and diverse.

I had recommended that only cream backing paper be used and that lots of mark making equipment was made available so that the children could create their own backgrounds and props. This had a direct and tangible impact on both their eagerness to mark make and the ownership of their play.

Reflections from the team

Visit number 1

Our school had been put forward to take part in a creativity project run by Alistair in order to support schools with promoting creativity in their environments and in the children's learning. I had recently attended a course run by Alistair and attended the Early Years Conference so was looking forward to Alistair's support and advice. I had already decided to deconstruct the role-play area as the one we had wasn't being used properly or by a large number and range of children. It had been mainly about girls role-playing with babies. After Alistair's initial visit we agreed to focus on the promotion of speech and language in our setting as it's of particular importance with our cohort of children.

To achieve the goal of children 'using their imaginations to re-create roles and experiences' and 'interact with each other taking turns in the conversation' as well as the use of language to form friendships, we decided that our area needed den making opportunities, more phones, enhancements linked to children's interests and opportunities for writing. Alistair drew up a plan of how the area would look and what resources we would need.

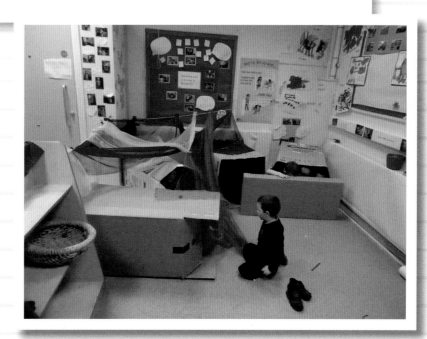

Visit number 2

Alistair brought with him some 'camping elastic' and I had purchased several lengths of different coloured voile materials. The elastic was used to section off an area and then it held the material in place in order to create a den. The lower walls were backed with plain paper and pens were provided. We had also sent out a request for any old mobile phones, so the children also had access to these, as Alistair had observed that children didn't necessarily want to give eye contact when they are not confident speakers - a phone enables them to engage in conversation or role-play without eye contact. As the den was completed the children immediately engaged with a wider variety of imaginary role-play and enjoyed the mark making on the wall. The boys in particular!

Visit number 3

Alistair surprised the children by introducing them to his ducklings. The children were very excited and asked lots of questions about the ducklings. This was an excellent speech and language opportunity for the children and was followed up with an activity linked to the question: 'Why don't their feathers get wet?' We talked about oil and water not mixing and made shakers containing oil and coloured water. The children's learning was extended further by encouraging children to time how long it would take for the oil and water to separate once shaken - an excellent opportunity to introduce the children to digital timers. The majority of children enjoyed this activity and although the timing wasn't always accurate the children were following the process correctly.

Impact

The deconstructed role-play is still working well and is used by all the children in the setting and for a wide range of purposes including, a hairdresser's and a boat! Large boxes have been used as cages, rockets and the children who do enjoy home corner role-play are still able to as those enhancements are still available to them. We are still learning how to improve our enhancements to encourage mark making, but most importantly for our setting is the fact that there is lots of imaginative language, interacting, negotiating, taking turns and forming friendships.

Our next steps are:

- to continue to enhance the deconstructed role-play, most importantly linked to children's interests.

- to focus on developing a range of speech and language opportunities throughout the setting including the 'Talk boxes'.

- to ensure planning is linked to children's interests to gain maximum engagement.

Case study 6

Project: **Den making**

Setting: A three-form entry primary school with a private nursery on site.

The brief:

This large primary school shares their large outdoor space with the private Nursery that is also on their site. The school has created a number of designated outdoor areas such as a garden and a track. They have also invested in some fixed outdoor play equipment such as a stage and a pirate ship. At the beginning of the project the three classes took it in turns to go out and use the outdoor play space. Due to the numbers of children and the added dimension of the Nursery, continuous outdoor provision was not in place.

Although the overall character of each class was completely different, there were common themes that arose when you looked at how they executed their outdoor play. Much of their play was very repetitive and always based around a few very familiar themes. This manifested itself most in the use of the pirate ship. Although the children clearly enjoyed playing on the ship, their play lacked any diversity. Every time they used it the role-play always reverted back to Peter Pan, with the same characters and the same story line.

On one visit to the setting I attempted to introduce another dimension to the Peter Pan play and was told in no uncertain terms that that WAS NOT how you played pirates. Of course it's good for children to create and consolidate familiar role-play. It makes them feel secure and builds their self-confidence because they know they can do it. When it can becomes an issue is if they just continue with that play scenario to the exclusion of anything else. We need to build on children's familiar play to expand their imaginations and open their minds to a range of other possibilities. The thing that I felt was most stifling their creative development was the use of the pirate ship. So, I wanted to work with the team to provide the children with an equally exciting but less structured option.

We decided on an outdoor den making project. The dens would be built by the children to their own specifications and for their identified purpose. As different children came to play in the den space the den could morph and change as the individuals who were in it introduced new dimensions to the play.

As the 'purpose' of the structure would not be fixed or obvious the children would have to communicate with each other and explain what the den was and what was happening. The very fact that it wasn't a particular 'something' would mean that it could be anything. It would all depend who was in it at the time.

The team identified a small strip of grass away from the other play equipment that they thought would be perfect. (Doing something with that strip of grass was a challenge in itself! Thank you!)

How it worked

The first task for the team was to collect as much 'cheap' den making equipment as they could. They did a brilliant job and we ended up with loads. My second visit to the setting was to work with the children to show them how to make a den using what we had. I wanted the children to be able to change the den and also repair it if it fell down, which it invariably would! We used mainly lengths of camping washing line, pegs, fabric and a few carpet inner tubes to provide height. This is the sort of activity that Nursery and Reception children are more than capable of doing on their own once they have been shown.

Usually, when I am den making with settings it is the boys who show the greatest interest but at this school it was the girls who were keenest to get stuck in and they mastered it very quickly. Initially the den play was around very familiar subject matter: house, bedroom, school, but within a very short space of time it began to change and grow.

One set of children would build and begin a play scenario but then some of them would leave and others would come. This resulted in threads of the original play being maintained whilst new dimensions were introduced by the children joining the play that changed its direction entirely. Like everything else, initially all of the children were really keen to have a go and experiment with den building but then when the novelty wears off you are left with a core of children who enjoy it. Other children are more inclined to revert back to the familiar play because they feel more secure with its familiarity and it's easier.

I did think on several occasions that you could turn your den into a pirate ship but your pirate ship is always a pirate ship and although it provides a strong scaffold for play, I have to question if ultimately it stifles it, especially where creative development is concerned. One of the interesting developments of this project was that the den making was not confined to the designated area or the Reception children. Inspired by the den making skills of the Reception children, the Nursery then turned part of their track into a car wash complete with foil water!

Also, as part of the project, we were keen to encourage the children to engage in mark making and art activities in their outdoor space, partly just to consolidate their mark making skills and partly to encourage the children to create 'props' to use in their play rather than just always choose the available familiar object. Our plan was to introduce a number of blackboards and art easels onto the outside walls. We also planned to put out a selection of natural materials and encourage the children to experiment to create their own transient artwork which would be photographed before the materials were returned for others to use. At the end of the project, this area was in its very emergent stages with all staff very keen to make it work.

Reflections from the team

Our focus was on den making and better organisation and use of the creative/mark making area in the outdoor area.

We identified a previously unused area for den making and bought new equipment suggested by Alistair to support this. As an adult led activity all the children were shown how to use the new equipment to make dens. By the end of the year the children were confident in using the resources by themselves to make their dens to enhance their play throughout the outdoor area. Even the Nursery children were keen to join in.

Another focus area outdoors was to develop their creative and mark making skills. This area was enhanced with a range of natural materials e.g. pebbles, shells, stones and wood. Following Alistair's guidance we purchased more easily accessible child-friendly storage. Developing these areas encouraged the children's imaginative play and further resources were added at the request of the children. As a result of these changes, children were able to demonstrate more imaginative role-play and more creativity with the resources.

The staff were very pleased with the children's responses. It was interesting to see how the three classes had very different approaches to the outdoor area. This showed the need for modelling of all areas/facilities initially, to then enable the children to extend their ideas and to attain the higher creative points.

In the new school year we have been given the enthusiasm to develop the outdoor creative curriculum further. We hope to use more of the school grounds using the local park ranger e.g. for the collection of leaves, seeds, branches etc to make natural dens.

Alistair gave us lots of ideas to use both indoors and outdoors.

An environment plan

Environment Plan

Setting name ....

Year ....

The purpose of this document is to clarify your thinking, and the thinking of your team, about why your setting looks the way that it does at different points during the year.

It should demonstrate clearly that your priority is to meet the particular needs of the children in your **CURRENT** cohort through your teaching and environment (indoors and out).

It should be a simple document that makes reference to other sources of evidence (do not rewrite what you have already written).

It should be updated once a term or when you make a significant change to your environment.

KEEP IT SIMPLE!

Ideas for sections and what to include

Section One: My space

Include photographs, pencil drawings, maps…whatever you feel most comfortable with that shows what your environment looks like. (Indoors and out).

Section Two: Autumn term set up

In this section list all of your areas in turn and describe how, and more importantly, WHY you have set them up in the way that you have.

What you have set up should be driven by assessment of the CURRENT cohort. If you have no assessment of the children you will be getting, then go with your prior knowledge of other cohorts on point of entry and what you know about skill development in children.

You need to record something along these lines:

Area: Mark Making (indoor)

- **I have placed my mark making area next to my dough area as there are a number of activities for emergent mark makers that utilise elements of both areas.**

- **There is a large clear floor area that allows for large-scale gross motor mark making as well as table top space for the development of fine motor work.**

- **I have specifically chosen resources for the shelving that will meet the needs of the children – identified by their last assessment (see assessment file July 2012).**

- **For my emergent mark makers I have…**

- **To develop pincer grip I have…**

- **For the development of fine motor movement I have…**

- **I have included a photograph for reference…**

This is a good activity for your whole team to do as it makes you ask yourself why you have a particular resource on the shelf. Also, don't be worried if your shelves look a little bit empty to start with (as long as you have a plan). You need to show children appropriate use of some equipment and often this means a staggered start to introducing all of the resources that you might have in mind.

Section Three: Spring term set up

As above – **SHOW** how you have made changes and **WHY.**

Section Four: Summer term set up

As above – **SHOW** how you have made changes and **WHY.**

In a different colour on your document show ONLY the changes you have made in each area, stating why. Include a Spring Term photograph for reference

Section Five: Does it work?

The only way that you will know if your environment is working is to stand back and look at it.

You need to regularly build in to your timetable opportunities to just stand back and look. To get a really good picture of the areas of your setting that are working well, you need observations to be done by a number of adults on a number of occasions at different times of the day.

Areas in use

Work shop		✓g	✓m	✓m	✓m	✓m	✓m
Card making	R						
Medal painting	Adult	–	✓m	✓b	✓g	✓m	–
Maths table	Adult R	✓	✓	✓	✓	–	✓
White board	Adult Y1	✓	✓	✓	✓	✓	–
Outdoor		✓	✓	✓	✓	✓	✓
Role-play writing table (Central)		✓g	–	✓m	–	–	–
Computer	R	✓m	–	✓m	✓g	✓m	✓m
Role-play	R	–	–	–	–	✓b	–
Sand (bay)		–	–	–	✓g	–	–
Construction role-play		✓m	–	–	–	✓g	✓m
Letter formation area		–	–	–	–	–	–
Reading	R	–	–	–	–	–	–
Water (bay)		–	–	–	–	–	–

These observations do not need to be pages and pages long they just need to tell you what is working well and who is accessing what.

This is a quick environment observation I did in a Reception/Year One setting. I listed all of the areas/activities and then visited each one every 15 minutes.

I gave a tick if there were children in the area and put a 'b' for boys 'g' for girls and 'm' for mixed. You can clearly see which areas are not being accessed. If this showed a pattern over time then you would need to address that use of space.

This is a crucial step which is often missed. When we are working with children we are often very involved in their play and we don't stand back and just look. Areas that provide high levels of engagement will always be well populated by children. You can see from one of these observations which areas are under-used but also if a particular gender group is dominating a specific space or activity. You can then amend your space or resourcing in response to your observations, assessments and children's preferences.

Outdoor

Farm play (real grass)	–	–	✓m	–	–	–
Maths (adult)	✓	✓	✓	✓	✓	✓
Reading (den)	✓	✓	✓	✓g	✓	✓
Sports day prac equipment	✓m	✓m	✓m	✓m	✓m	✓b
Tent with books	✓g	✓m	✓g	–	–	✓g
Home made skittles (adult)	✓	✓	✓	✓	✓	✓
Drawing (mark making table)	✓m	–	–	✓g	–	✓b
Garage	✓	✓	✓	✓	✓b	✓b
Shell exploration	–	–	–	–	–	–
Water play	✓b	–	–	–	–	✓g